Dancing on Main Street

POEMS BY

Lorenzo Thomas

COFFEE HOUSE PRESS

2004

Coffee House Press books are available to the trade through our primary distributor, Consortium Book Sales & Distribution, 1045 Westgate Drive, Saint Paul, MN 55114. For personal orders, catalogs, or other information, write to: Coffee House Press, 27 North Fourth Street, Suite 400, Minneapolis, MN 55401. Good books are brewing at coffeehousepress.org.

Coffee House Press is a nonprofit literary publishing house. Support from private foundations, corporate giving programs, government programs, and generous individuals help make the publication of our books possible. We gratefully acknowledge their support in detail in the back of this book.

ACKNOWLEDGMENTS

Some of these poems have previously appeared in *African American Review, The Art Journal, Bayou Review, Bombay Gin, Boog City, Callaloo: A Journal of African-American and African Arts and Letters, Chain, The Floating Bear, Gulf Coast: A Journal of Literature and Fine Arts, Hambone, i.e. Magazine, Kente Cloth: African American Voices in Texas, Long News in the Short Century, Lungfull!, The New Censorship, New Texas, The Paris Review, Poetics Journal, Poetry Project Newsletter, Project Papers, ¡Tex!, Texas Observer, Umbra, The World,* and *Xavier Review.* "Back-Ordered Tears" was originally published in *Ploughshares.*

"Dangerous Doubts" was included in *Roundup: An Anthology of Texas Poets,* ed. Dave Oliphant (Cedar Park: Prickly Pear Press, 1999). "Displacement" appeared in *The Paris Review Anthology,* ed. George Plimpton (New York: W. W. Norton, 1990). Some of these poems have also appeared in the chapbook *Magnetic Charms* (Camden: Walt Whitman Cultural Arts Center, 2002); and in *There Are Witnesses/Es Gibt Zeugen* (Eggingen and Hamburg: Edition Klaus Isele, 1996), a collection in the bilingual OBEMA series. Grateful acknowledgment is given to the editors of these publications.

Special thanks to Ivan Suvanjieff and Lee Christopher of *The New Censorship,* Charles H. Rowell of *Callaloo,* Thomas Bonner, Jr. of *Xavier Review,* Alicia Askenase and David A. Kirschenbaum, and Wolfgang Karrer at Universität Osnabrück.

LIBRARY OF CONGRESS CATALOGING-IN-PUBLICATION DATA

Thomas, Lorenzo
Dancing on Main Street : poems / by Lorenzo Thomas.—1st ed.
p. cm.
ISBN 1-56689-156-6 (alk. paper)
1. City and town life—Poetry. 2. Panamanian Americans—Poetry. I. Title.
PS3570.H568D36 2004
811'.54—DC22 2004000680

Contents

[Mister Anderson]

Any Place You've Ever Been

11 The Kite and the Hawk
12 South St. Blues
14 Please, Don't Let Me Be Misunderstood
15 When If the Big Bands Come Back
16 Guerrilla Girls
18 Displacement
21 Sentiment
25 Suburban Saturdays
27 Morning Raga
29 The Audie Murphy Game

Rituals & Improvisations

33 Destruction of the Seated Man
35 Last Call
39 Excitation
44 Skunk Insulation
46 Grudge Match
47 Lifelong Learning
49 Otis
52 Spirits You All
58 Journey of 1,000 Li
60 Tirade

The Simplest of All Mysteries

63 Poem in Lieu of the Marriage of Andrew Zolem

65 The Sadness of Space Exploration

66 Quiet Riot

67 Dumb Luck

69 The New South

71 Lights Out

72 No, Don't Get Up

73 The Failure of Alchemy

74 Working-Class Hero

75 The Gambler

76 Knight to Queen's Pawn

77 An Old Hand

78 Pornography = Exploitation of Men

81 Now You Can Worry

83 L'Argent

Resistance as Memory

87 Thinking in Words

90 Like a Tree

93 Sightseeing in East Texas

95 Psalm

100 Back in the Day

103 Whale Song

104 Songs Without Shadows

108 The Marks Are Waiting

112 Dirge for Amadou Diallo

115 An Afternoon with Dr. Blumenbach

Dangerous Doubts

119   Dangerous Doubts

120   Lustre

121   Cameo in Sudden Light

124   Country Song

125   Multicultural

126   Low Rider

127   An Even-Tempered Girl Holds Her Breath

128   She Lived to Be 100

129   A Kind of Accounting

131   Cute Girl with a Toy Monkey

133   Flash Point

134   God Sends Love Disguised as Ordinary People

136   Magnetic Charms

138   Equinox

144   Back-Ordered Tears

Mister Anderson
would always tell us that

if a black man
is the first
to cross your doorstep
New Year's

        you have good luck
             all year long

   Each New Year day was
earlier eyes for him

Up & down our block
he'd go knocking
on sleepy neighbors'
        doors

   Mister Anderson was not the sort
of man

     to leave
his neighborhood's good fortune
    up to chance

Any Place You've Ever Been

"*The earlier religions had their myths interpreted by means of the oral and unwritten Wisdom. We have ours* misinterpreted; *and a great deal of what has been imposed upon us as God's direct, true, and sole revelation to man, is a mass of* inverted myths, *under the shadow of which men have been cowering as timorously as birds in the stubble, when a kite in the shape of a hawk is held hovering overhead to keep them down. . . .*"

—GERALD MASSEY

The Kite and the Hawk

Man is no longer alone in the universe!

The day I found the hieroglyphic formula
For happiness for all mankind
I had to promise to give it away.

It is we have to find a way
For everyone to have
One more of something
Than your neighbor has

For you—here is a dollar!

And for you,
I feel warm brotherhood
And love intense
Beyond what anyone has ever felt before.

You didn't think I'm going around
And giving everybody money?

For me
The syllable of antique power
To shift the Light above
Enough to cast the second or third shadow
The Grand Prize
In the lottery of loneliness

South St. Blues

South St., you know, is not on any map.
There's just a bending line, a littered street.
It might even be a mental region.
So many faces, black, so occupied with pain and others,
just as painfully, a frozen blank.
I thought I'd crash out once (I'd seen a movie),
turned faintly philosophic, spoke at synagogues.
I'd try to talk away the taste of pigmeat
in my mouth, passing along South St. on the bus, eyes closed:
"I'm Palance dying for the thousandth time, on the
crags, name of his woman on his lips,
a letter to her, painfully writ, in his pocket. The pain
we bear before making it! Almost a requisite, the
coldness, even those crags."

But Palance wouldn't do. Fugitive, I come and stroke your
hair. I smile at you. You wonder where my
eyes are. I fix my mind on you, say: "It's hard
to understand." You're only human,
want to know your stature in my eyes. Stand here, look for
my eyes, sun at your back. You'll see.
I take you without thought, trying to banish
South St. from my mind. But the days reel off like old film,
unwanted moments bang against the brain. In your

face a stolen lyric can be read, a medieval tune full
of eastern Europe, the long nights with dark
and contemplative men, the midnight pogrom.
Tune for clarinet and balalyka, violin.
You don't know why it makes me sing my kind of blues.

Please, Don't Let Me Be Misunderstood

—AFTER EDGAR CAIRO

You vex me so
Impatient sigh,
Land whose liberation waits
In my own breath

Your distant yearning
Forces my conscience to protest

Word upon word
Whirls to a hurricane
Inside me

Your heavy sighs
Your whisperings
Spiral around that place
Where I must tug
Myself
To thread the sandbars of my nation's peace

My heart lists in the flood
As my blood churns

Please don't accuse me of embittered exile,
Mother. Don't call me a motherless child

When ~~If~~ the Big Bands Come Back

Love fills its absences with doubt
And nights with fruitless pain
Knits its brow to wring a problem
Out. Love seeds its care with rain.

Love feels departure's space
With some of the most incredible
Foolishness. Like sombreros
Purchased on a trip to Santa Fe

Greenwich Village African bracelets

Fading photographs that are mislaid
In strange places far from the place
The loved one and the lover were
Ever really together. The daily mail.

But we have to put up with it
Our most popular songs are composed
They Can't Take That Away From Me

I'll write you "Every Day I Have the Blues"

Guerrilla Girls

Harbor road is handily lifted
A summer waiting in the sky
Foreigners crowd the landings
She tells me of the Nazi death camp,

Some of them the blondes feed
Me bread and safe water
And it is better than nothing.
"How you feel Joe"
She says she was born near San Reys.

Ulla's silk and rayon shift
Repeats properly
Oceans the mind busy positioning
The operation is repeated
Many times per second
Bending down beside the groaning oars
Outside the long shed

Speech,
A receiver continuously responsive and capable

Birds condense in her wool mouth
Underneath her throat knots of recognition.
Can you be busted for fucking
The enemy? The radio is curiously
Still in the tropical night

The walkie-talkie is shadowed
And morose. Just like a spring
Which released, goes beyond its usual
Position and then returns,

She releases me from politics
Inside a socialist novel
Which released, goes beyond
Its usual position and then returns, just like
That bathing suit model on the dais at Saks

Displacement

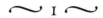 I

To a lotus beaming in the grime

Behind the house,

The light is very clear

The parasol is painted

We moving
Guy at the
Wheel sd
"I see
They got it
Finished" But
Nothing is
Finished.

Every day someone returns
To the field

Before his wanting becomes a rainbow
He must pause.

The waters rise up
In a dull sheaf

As if miracles were due

But it is only
The harvest;
Only the buffalo's bulk
In the water

The new figure of Buddha beside the road
Between Phu Xuan and Tan Thuan Dong
Shivering in the cold
Flood of vast brown sky

 II

Wish you were heir
To more naturalness
Than simple lust
For daily bread and restaurants
Where the waiters
Still speak French

Wish you could hear more
In the dark

More than crickets
Your grandfather's cough
Or the songs of
The little fishes

Listen. This is modern times all over the world

Go sit under a tree.

Who studies the physics
Of nonentities?

A facsimile becoming a disguise

Who is not supposed to be reading
This postcard

I am pleased to surprise the people
Any afternoon

And those who do not
Care to understand
That I know. You know.

Everywhere it is the same thing
Only different.
High officials
Flash by
Hostaged in their
Entourage.

She told me I'm glad
We are not important
We can go walk around
And sit in cheap
Cafés by the road.

SAIGON, VNCH 1971

Sentiment

Grander designs for the living room paper
And the full, bright sound of the daylight
Came to touch some Thing in our thoughts
Of the misleading vacations. We blanked
And felt the force of our garments
This language that rinses in our flesh
Waterfalls coloring the air wide for identification
Our discussions at the Federal office for that
And information more irrelevant in the streets
In the end, it would only remind us
Once again the dry weekend in Boston
Hearing "Satisfaction" in the bar
Coming over the television out some
Skinny and casual illusion
The temporary grace of being in business
That the whole world surrounds
A dull sensation, like standing
Over a long empty bar drinking
Martinis at midnight just for fun
And create the unusual for Boston

Any place you have ever been still responds
To the rhythm of your illusion

REVEAL NEW INFORMATION settles there
Under the feet of the people bored
Returning from the financial world
Into soft decades of crime and world

War like a curtain across the rooms
The sane rooms. And in a room picked
At random somewhere across Boston
She is pouring water from one bowl
Into another to dye her hair gold

Where I walk in with directions and purpose
Putting slugs in cigaret machines there
Smoking and watching TV thinking abt you
This song wd be lost there in Boston,

Under my feet more startling disclosures
And I could go on singing almost forever!

Of course not.

                          Until that song falls down

                  There is nothing
                    So beautiful

The form of artifice destroys itself
Axxxx xxx xfxxx xxxxxxxxxx rx xxxx
xxxxxxxx xxxx xxxxx it is as if you
Had stolen away to the river some calm
(Good!) but the river was flushing 300 red-
Faced conventioneers to the Falls

And cared to do nothing about this!

Thinking: it will be good for at least half
A page in the scrapbook you misplaced

DREDGE RIVER FOR CONVENTION BODIES

Thinking it will be worth six good words
Over dinner of baked macaroni and meat-
Balls with a mushroom and onion gravy sauce
And black coffee served in classical cups

I am ashamed of that Good. The slow down trip
The mirrors of a music box settled
On "The Inventions" some such golden
Racket annoyance lace organic satins

Pink bunched up around the doll
Who sits in the album and
Worries about the sunlight
Of years already forgotten

Lost in the old corners of deshabille peasant
Evenings with the same old wallpaper and
Same old dull slide show white boys meet
White girls at the Charles white bicycles

Washed by the elegant light playing it up and
Flicker in the room where a woman
Puzzles her mirror with the chemical dream
Turning herself into a photo of old Boston

What you said, and almost collapsing back into the rum

And the sky so open this morning
No such thing as the Mediterranean
Only the smell of trees in Boston
Sunlight in her new ridiculous hair

Under my feet. More startling disclosures.
And I could go on singing almost forever!

Of course not.

Suburban Saturdays

Given choices, standing in the street
And shouting
Even for a worthy cause
The way we used to do
When we were young
Even for nothing
Is not choice

The world has changed.

Homely estrangements
In the presence of one's children
Is more fun
Less public and, embarrassing to say, less private
Even.
           You're weeping through
The Way We Were on cable
They are saying, "Huh?
I don't like Barbra Streisand anyway
Her nose is funny"
                They have no time for you
No words and infinitely less concern
They vanish after dark
Just like you taught them to at 3
But now it hurts.

All parents reach this point, a cliff.
Maturity is what we like to call it

The world has changed
Manners your elders strapped you into
Somehow have come unraveled in your hands
You watch the loose ends
Flap away like thoughtless tongues
Dances, movies, parties
Impudent and bold, and beautiful
And realize, that given choices,
Had you known,
It really wouldn't have turned out this way

Morning Raga

While you slept undoubtedly
Some tragedy occurred
And the dismal muezzins
Of the half-past modern
Western world begin to chatter
Powdered and grave
Wrapping the world
In a one-size-fits-all demise
Provided for promotional considerations

But somewhere someone
Is watching *Orphée Noir*
Thinking Jobim is wonderful
And thinking how great it must be
To believe someone must sing
A song to bring the sun
Up

While those happily tangled hesitate
Confusing duty with a slow myopic scanning
Of the single face
That captures all the brand-new light
Releasing it one eyelash at a time

As students giggle riding on a train through Tyrol
Missing islanded monasteries from the guidebook
But not the real smell of sheep and swine

Beside the roadbed as the train slows down
Sliding into and out of flowered little towns

And somewhere where it is already yesterday
Or still tomorrow
In just a little while
Someone will say:

While you slept undoubtedly
Some tragedy occurred
If you think you'll be happier
That way, starting your day
Believe them

But some
Where some
One is
Singing.

The Audie Murphy Game

When I was an infant playing
With myself I dreamed of Fame

Being an infantry hero being in movies
Recounting my patriot murders
Playing myself. Drunkenly driving
To death if need be to fulfill

This legend in my own time. Tsk tsk.
When I discovered I could not
Win the Vietnam war I couldn't
Be a hero dammit I couldn't wear

The Congressional Medal of Honor
I was very disappointed. I cried
To the gods for a second chance

And the gods cried back "no way buddy"

Rituals & Improvisations

Destruction of the Seated Man

—AFTER DE KOONING'S *Seated Man*
CA. 1938, NOW DESTROYED

 I

bloodless hands glowing
staring at each other's emptiness
postured as if expecting
something to hold
wistful apprehension
the lines of the face
could be disbelief fascination?
suspended fear maybe anxiety
of impending whirlwinds
the boiling shadows
eat at the flesh
and shining hands too weak
to grasp eternity
wait for it to fall into their
upturned palms.

II

perhaps those eyes are
watching some color splashed smeared
abstraction of the Landing
or the silent cool night-beauty—
sky lit with a distant neon rainbow

watching the vermilion montage of morning
rape the trembling nightness

 III

the penetrating darts
through the shoulders
later tore off the shadow-bitten
head sent it spinning thru the
electrified landscapes of Death
the man still sat in the bright vacantness
some of us can make our world
blackwhite and sit headless with waiting hands
forever

1962

Last Call

In *The Odyssey*, Book IX, we learn of a fierce battle with the Ciconians on the island of Ismaros:

> *From that place we sailed onward much discouraged, but glad to have escaped death, although we had lost good companions. Yet we did not let the galleys go off, until we had called thrice on the name of each of our hapless comrades who died in that place.*
> —*THE ODYSSEY*, TR. W. H. D. ROUSE

Erwin Rohde, in *Psyche*, comments: "References to similar callings upon the dead in later literature make the meaning of such behaviour clear. The souls of the dead who have fallen in foreign lands must be 'called'; they will then, if this is properly done, follow the caller to their distant home, where an 'empty grave' awaits them."

This poem is about veterans of the war in Viet Nam.

> *If anybody's carrying a rabbit's foot, hang on to it tight.*
> —VAN JOHNSON IN *30 SECONDS OVER TOKYO*

Corned beef sandwiches, water, plenty
Of time to think about the future
You too can grow up to be a square-jawed
American hero, eyes rounding up with recognition
That horror that looked so darn familiar
Really knows you. Grew up in the same town
And memorized the same stupid movies.

It's just us now, huddled in the same apprehension
That whatever is outside this bubble
Is probably no stranger. It gets harder
To swallow, the temperature's rising,
The lies and the half-truths go whistling by

Stand by
For voices blending into stridency
Practiced as alarms
This is the daily danger
We would stay awake,
Missing nothing. Clear the head.
There is some place now

Just as it materializes on this page
Or fills the ear of the peaceful sleeper

Familiar
As a song that has been on the radio
About six weeks, the smile a little grayer
But the same no-nonsense haircut,
And the words of the heartbroken girl
Making sense. Suddenly, clear the head!

It's me Clothilde!

What are you afraid of? The fires behind us
Are our signatures. Our memories cannot harm us,
Unless we allow them to talk to our friends
And anyone who'd believe them is not really a friend.

Oh poo, she teases.
You have been lax
Don't you remember me
Your pretty little America
Blue and shimmering

Around the corner is a warm and cozy place
Complete with lovable and laughing folks
Waiting in a kind of strange suspenseful animation
For us. To just appear and be ourselves is all
They live for. Anticipation of our beauty
Keeps them lifelike, poised, waiting for your call.
You see? These are your memories.
They will say what you want them to say
And amuse you. They will whine and cower,
Backbite you into the most heartless, unfeeling
Wretch the world has ever known
The most untrustworthiest son of a bitch
The most thankless, loving serf of humanity
Most sweetest, kindest, cut-throat whatever
Until you are happy. See? What are friends for?

Let's get it on before big sister comes.
We dare not admit even suspicions of failure
It is better not to even begin.
And no time wasted on remember when.
I think the truth might be a little prettier
With a bit of stainless steel and neon
Over here. Maybe some glass bricks.
A miniature rain forest in the bath
Sounds a lot better than pipes that drip all night

Our hearts are blessed with an efficient fancy
Corned beef sandwiches, water, plenty
Reasons to be happy in love. So we didn't know
Where we were going, but we are finally here!
A carnival of soft-spoken meanness
Welcomes you to your new refrigerator carton
And honored place among the lowest middle-class

Gee, you look so familiar

Excitation

O wondrous thing it is
Oh what a wondrous thing it is
We often thought, to live
Through the senses
When they quicken and stir at even

One
Assays kaleidoscopes of failing light
Another
Revels in the moist kiss of the night
Approaching

        soon enough chased,
The kiss, by the dry scentlessness of central heat
So Prussian, so precise

          When nature struggles against artifice
In a madly sensuous pas de deux
Lovely as the chevrons of late traffic
Dancing across high ceilings, cooling walls
Fleeting to sight yet permanent
In the mind's storage place of kinetics
To be unwrapped some day when words fail
And, like any forgotten bundle in a warehouse
Puzzling because no one remembers what they were
What use they serve
Where did this stuff come from?

Or even how the hell it got here
Such simple-minded mysteries can make your day

ALL OF THIS IS A CERTIFIED EXCERPT FROM A DREAM. THERE WERE SPIRITS
HOVERING OVER OR AS IN THE OLD LANGUAGE'S SIGNS "UP ABOVE MY HEAD"
A SPECIAL SORT OF MUSIC IN THE AIR . . . SOMETHING THAT WAKES YOU UP
JUST LIKE SUNLIGHT
LIKE A PHONECALL AT DAWN
15 MINUTES BEFORE THE ALARM GOES OFF
A ROUGH AND ROLLING MUSIC
LIKE 1940S BLUES
WHISKEY & WOMEN AND ALL THE OTHER JIVE
THE JIVERS KNEW
ALL THE SINGERS OF SENSE WHO HAD NO SENSE
OR ELSE THEY WOULDN'T HAVE BEEN SINGING
"WELL, YOU KNOW . . . "

The permutations,   or
                    just   listening
         Roscoe Gordon
                             Peppermint
      "I Been Booted"
                    or is it " . . . just got
         FAT GIRL BOOGIE
                    & sordid ordered trash
         The permuted sounds
         of a special estranged English
         And who in hell
                    and this is it, if nowhere else
will ever ever understand
That all of these cats
                    were Charles Brown

yes, even
    Nat "King" Cole
urbane and suave
           his pictures in the best of JET
In those pulp days, pulp times
A hundred years past slavery still
The same old shuffle
        In Alabama, where the redneck fans
    attacked poor Nat on stage   just like Roland Hayes
      knocked him down, down to the ground
    sd, "Nigger!"

Such raw country voices, the Ku Klux Klan meets Rhythm & Blues

IT SOUNDS LIKE THIS: Byebye, bye
        Baby
          byebye
    Oh what a wondrous thing
        I think it is
    But goddam baby
        baptist to the heart
I'm getting tithed of you, momma
    But I love, Lord knows
    most as much as I loves
          myself

AND LOST LOTS OF FOOLS

MOANING & GOING ON   (in the background)

Certainly, this should awaken the mind
And the senses should shut down in shame
But it is such a lovely clear break in the day
Only a fool who would remain a fool
Would have the nerve to shoo this shoofly away

"Anytime you bother me, bubba . . . "
But, momma,
You
Can bother the heck
Out of me!

               If you were me
            Or anywhere
                              by me
               Or near,
         Baby baby baby
         What a scene this cd be here
                  Oh baby baby baby
               And lots of lost fools
               Moaning & going on   (way in the background y'know)
                  Just like church   way back
                        in the wildwood
                     just like in the arbor
                        somewhere just outside
               And lost fools
                  just like church   way back
                        in the wildwood
            moaning & going on
                  like in de brush arbor
                     somewhere just outside
               up   down
               back of town

So much to say, we negroes here
Oh yes, we've had some fun
Have sang the blues and did what had to be done
We often thought, to live
O what a wondrous thing
Fleeting to sight yet permanent
To sit despised on the outskirts of your town
Black fat deprived & jap-eyed
Yes, we sing. "Baby baby baby, why you?"
When nature struggles against artifice
To be unwrapped some day when bullshit fails
And, like any forgotten bundle in a warehouse
Lovely as the chevrons of late traffic
So Prussian, so precise
Like a phonecall at dawn from your baby
Moaning & going on . . .
Such simple-minded mysteries can make your day

The jivers knew
All all of these acts
Were Charles Brown's
A rough and rolling music
Just like sunlight
Just like Church
Fleeting to sight yet permanent
To be unwrapped some day
When words fail
What use they serve
Or else they wouldn't have been
Singing

Skunk Insulation

Random
As any Oklahoma
Rundown
As a long black silence
Roadway
Slicing vacancies
And separations
u.s. Highway metronome
Into tick-thuds
Of wheels on asphalt

All a formal invitation to the jolt

You can roll up the windows
                            don't work
Light up a Camel
                            don't work
Believe I say, do you BELIEVE
In even a roadkill Heaven
Where there's never
Any traffic anymore
To fan and flutter your
Conscience swooning ease
                            won't work

Act tough
Until
The tears burst
From your ears

           will do no good

No brutish plan, no choice of sin
Can tip a karmic scale
No euphemisms of passion
Or vampired politeness
Could make any difference,

For 2.5 miles or 3 minutes
You could
Hold your breath
Try for a record

           or simply admit it

Nothing gives up this world
Without a comment

Grudge Match

Mocking as sunrise
To insomniacs
As painfully predictable
Is a resentful child
Who boldly signs her mother's malady
Wishing a womb again
Curls into silences
And flames with mute disdain
Her empty-headedness
Provides a constant echo
Of Dad's failures

A healthy family might shout
And rage their way through this
To an embrace of sanity.
At least, civility.
A wealthy one would pack her off to school
Hoping
That somewhere in a corner of this earth
Another pair has built a boy
To match this fool

Lifelong Learning

One day my Dad
Decided
Whatever else we were in life
We should be rich

I don't like being poor
He said, I don't like
Getting up at 4 o'clock dark
Day after day
2 subways to somebody's job
To put 3 dollars every week
Into a Christmas Club
And after scrimp and save and all

What come
The end of every month
The same rob Peter
To pay Paul

There's got to be a better way

The scheme he fell for was a scam
"Direct mail"
Was the road we chose
To riches

We sent away for
Mailing lists, ordered a crate of doohickeys
Printed 1,000 flashy ads
Return address embossed
The name we picked
H. HAMILTON RICKARD & SONS
Would sound to suckers like we'd been
In business for a century

"Purveyors of fine doohickeys"

We didn't do so well
Of course
A small fortune in stamps was lost
By Christmas
No cash left to shop
We did the best
With what we'd got:
Doohickeys went to all our friends.

What never broken never mends

Otis

Some women think
A man should hunt for them

Some women understand it

And some men think
Return a wondrous thing

She must be waiting

The dude goes out,
Is gone all night
She knits and yearns
Till gray dawnlight
Her girlfriends say,
"That trifling
                    blank
Ain't coming back"
And help her undo her
                              work

That's the kind of cat,
You know,
"No man can take
My place"
Instantly trucks his shadow
Through the door

Catches a fit
That blinds him
Even further.

Folks like that
You hear about them
On the News.

Some women understand it

Another dude,
You know,
Is gone for days
But she sits, humming
At first a moan
She knits and polishes
And frets.
She frowns at friends
Then sings a gleeful song
As they fidget them
Whisper, "Girl,
Is you gone mad?"
So all of them chorusing
"That trifling
                    blank
Um hmmm, I knows
                    a man!"

Some women

Man, by the time
My man tipped in
She had damn near enough
Macramé string
To make a hammock
That sleep two
                on top
Three on the
                bottom

Some women
              think
And there is beauty
In the knit
            of thinking

Some dudes know
How to treat a woman
Right

Some don't

Some women understand it

Spirits You All

THE CHARLES GAYLE TRIO AT THE HOUSTON JAZZ FESTIVAL,
SEPTEMBER 16, 1992
——FOR CHARLES GAYLE

All it is

Church

If you hear it

He
Church

He
Concerthall flame breath
To sidewalk
Breathes
Through a saxophone
To deep pulsing tunnels
The people
Whipped by the money changers
Beat down by money
Hang wearily
Awaiting darkness
Bats

He church

Speaking no words
Their souls are not silent
He
Makes audible
The sonar of thousands
The horn coaxes measured Jesus
Sing
Gayle,
Angular
Erect
Vattel Cherry dances
Bass
Bells like the click of cowries
Flash like sparks
Around his instrument
Marc
Edwards reaches
For a distant drumbeat
Snaring it, then lets
It go
To fly around this space

Inside his saxophone
Are all the voices
Spirits you all
The shrieks of Daddy Grace
And grandmaw's moan

Young girls
All that is truly precious of the earth
Loud and laughing

Who do not know
The troubles of this world
Glowing
With bells in their ears
Fluttering bird-like
In girl conspiracies

From concerthall under red lights
To sidewalks exiled from neon

If you can hear it
Spirits you all
Dance from this saxophone

Cold light in falling darkness

Under the shudder of Suburbans
Fuming on the overpass
A woman in a carton
She might have asked a husband
To break down
And stack beside the drive for heavy trash
Busies her hands
Folding rags with gracious care
Into a plastic bag

Her heart just idles
And her mind curls up
Around a picture of a small white clapboard
Missionary Baptist Church
Nestled in hope beside a county road

Where the choir voice
Was all the sound of life
To laughing girls
And soft brown faces
Some of them softened only
When they sang

Church don't mean religion
May even be a verb

Sleeping in fits
A man ten feet away
Wrapped in a sheet of cardboard
Does not dream;
That lobe was leached
In floods of liquid flame
That made 1,000 nights like this
Instant forgettings
And survivable
He does not see himself
In marcelled hair
Long gleaming Stacy Adams cordovans
As dangerous as German u-boats
On the Dreamland floor
As the orchestra
High trumpet, hoarse trombones
Slides into "Cherry Pink
And Apple Blossom White"

You think these cracked feet
Have no mambo memory?

Well, no they don't
He never did that
But he saw it in a movie once
A century ago

He
Church in trembles

Joy?

And struggle

Jjjoy and and struggle

Here
Where night's a cloak
Of heavy hopelessness
And day a flash of puzzled patterns
Lining it
A fashion
Such ill-fitting materiality
That even those who grab the most
See themselves scrambling
To barely cover their behinds

And now the brazen shofar of a horn
As the commuter bats
Unfold themselves into
The evening
And step along the sidewalk

And do not look around or down
And if they do don't see
What you can hear
Spiraling out of Charles Gayle's saxophone
Spirits you all

Know where it comes from

Church if you feel it

Journey of 1,000 Li

It's as if all my memory
Is still on decks of cards

Everyone else has chips
Shuffled carelessly

Blue-backed diamonds ending up
In a red deck

Where I expected Christmas 1949 to be
Phone numbers

Though "Sunday Morning" always is
Exactly where it's always been

It's playing havoc with my *Pensées*
Which ought to be

Bright insights based on turns
Of clever sayings

Polished to delight
By life's experiences

What never dims, though
Is your specialness

Beloved, if we were in China
I'd owe you my life

Or is it have to teach you
How to fish

Tirade

Now I know old age is cruel
It brings fears you never knew

There is a hazard in the morning sun,
A thirty percent chance
This day will pass without
The birth of a regret
Or the blossoming of a sorrow
So well behaved and mild
Shyly, patiently
Gaining courage all these years
Blurting into the bliss
You've sown around you

These passions make your life last longer
Waiting for the day
You can no longer push them away.
Arms weakened,
Your heart grows stronger
And wisdom clinging to you like a child
To her broken doll,
You may finally sort everything out
And end with nothing
Left to fear tomorrow

The Simplest of All Mysteries

Poem in Lieu of the Marriage of Andrew Zolem

We met like songs say in a cellar café
Maybe we were sad   we were smoking
Thinking of your living room flowery laughter
And the ladies coming by to play mah-jongg

To have been brought up here, a house with books
And someone vaguely remembering great music
During unusual moments when pruning the hedge
Gallantly shuffling toward the new bed

He takes off the dark cape-like robe revealing
Black silk pajamas   Leaps tenderly into
The white folds of the bridge and thinks and
Comes, is it the harlot of "Clair de Lune"

Is it the tacky innocence of Debussy now waking up now
Here on the chest and the arms of the custom
Where the recent past returns, the rear guard of
The white flowers serenades and card games

Blackjack in the fat parlor after her family
Had gone to bed. Softly touching his hand
When it was her turn to deal   Or playing whist
Trump trump   pawed over the small table.

Then the parents would come in with their lies
Or cough from their sloppy insomniac bed
Thinking of her sluffing it off at breakfast
Don't you think I know you know I care

The table with the two different death services
Livery and tambourines on the one hand
Even though she lived in a bourgeois comm-
Unity built on the expected assent

We ignore when these white designs are brought to the room
And evil marriage, virtuous as a lab attendant
Comes up out of the phonograph just like "La Mer"
Out of all the white vases like soft dallying

Which is not literature or the social structure
Which is not the province of the first night
Now, now sleep reigns contrary to the caveat
Emptor of our Jewishness and careful instructions

We realize that we are no longer aware of Spain
Its sunlight and love songs. Our wedding
Night has been unnecessary like no songs say.
With your ring we have aborted our children

And our youth shuffles toward the dusty encyclopedia
That we will have to buy them, toward sex books
You will find under their pillows   tsk tsk
The theme of Faro explains your lover's death

It is all there, cached in your stupid new husband.
Children will dig it up to sell you subscriptions
You could have had those beautiful, sly little bastards
Know it, Orpheus sends back your regards.

1965

64

The Sadness of Space Exploration

——FOR KAREN

We must never grow up
If all we learn is kindness

Not making promises
We may not know how to keep
Is both affection and an immaturity
That baffles feelings
Amid the circus clamor
Of a pleasant village day
Humid with rituals and schoolkids

Because passion is a need beyond desire
His matinee-style courtliness
Is matched by her astonished grace

Two gleeful children hide in them
Under the shadows of heaven
Deciphered and confused again
Beneath fidgeting trees.

Quiet Riot

I'd rather not negotiate
An understanding

I have no taste
For anorexic conversations
Without your richly-layered innuendo
Or parables of just desserts
Among acquaintances

If you really have something to say
It's worth breaking out the good china

Put the damn tin cup away

Dumb Luck

Because
I could not fix my mouth to say
I need you so
You saw me coming

When you have lived so long
Your only prayer
Is Lord, please
Give me one more clear
Indignity to magnify
That length of suffering
Becomes the latest fashion
With transatlantic fortunes riding
On a hem,

In the moon-rinsed
Casinos of romance
I gamed and lost.

Wrong choice
Of games.
Stammers
Of pride

And 3 unanswered hearts

No time left
For the simple dice-toss
Of a plain apology.
And, in the end
I could not raise a hand
Against you

The New South

A sentimental drunkard
Don't you know
"Cottage For Sale"
3 a.m. Vegas lonely standard time
Brought me to tears

Impoverished no way
Except mementos
Daydream afternoons
Of make-believe old age
And modest wealth

The way things ought to be

I lusted for the luxury
Imagine
To have a shuttered witness
To a year we lived on Art and lentils
Joyously

In (of all places) Pine Bluff, Arkansas
The house we loved in
Owned by a cracked belle
Who had the place torn down
The month we moved

An attitude
Just a little more extreme
Than your own mother's
Who only said, Make sure
You don't keep grass around the house

You two have enough problems

Lights Out

It's not that I've grown blind
To your attractions
Or that your beauty
Is enhanced by candlelight
The way Frank Capra
Rubbed petroleum jelly on the lens
To make us yearn
Until a held breath
Clenches our hearts
For Barbara Stanwyck

But, as you say
It's not that how we feel
About each other is so new
Or special like it has never
Been an overworked cliché
Happened to us or anyone
Before (even in movies)
But, really very simply
Diminishing distractions
Never hurts

No, Don't Get Up

I watched her throw
Her ribbons on the floor
She put her foot down.
I asked her, as she turned
Toward the door
"Where will you go?"
"Crazy," she answered
"And I insist on driving myself."

The Failure of Alchemy

What love accounts for
In this day and time
Trusted somewhat less than safety

    A bond that ensures

Tears
Even if counterfeit
Earn interest

    Yet and still

There comes a day
Weary of starving greed
True love goes blind

And leaves a wife who could be good

Stumbling through chores
Vacuuming his pockets
Heart and mind.

Working-Class Hero

Some days feels like
You wake up underwater
It isn't the humidity I'm talking about

Space folds on space. A blue icehouse.
And every motion climbs into itself
A little man in someone else's overcoat

Some days are Sunday all day long
Below an empty sky that's eyeball blue
A slight wind curling round you like a vine

A day to put your bag on the conveyor belt
And walk on through

What kind of day today?
You could just say
I really didn't need something
To tell my grandkids

The Gambler

Took a note on my house in Ozone Park
That's why I'm out here working
I don't need to be out here you know
I did something I know I shouldn't do
Gave 27,000 to my kids

The boy's OK,
Though.
Smooth as Chinese silk
A engineer
Married to a Philadelphia gal
My wife don't care
For her, but she's OK

My girl's in school getting a masters
That's why I'm out here working

That girl,
I knew it from the first
My son's little girl, too

They was born to break hearts

Knight to Queen's Pawn

I married you because
You said you
Loved to cook
A gamelan of 3rd grade mischief
In your voice enchanted me
And I was hungry.

I married you
Because you swore to God
You were blond all over

Well
Your wealthy uncle
Who was set to croak
At any minute
Is now 112 years old

Your promises are dulled by overuse
And neither of us has set hearts-a-singing

Still
If we have nothing left
But carnal beauty

Well, I can live with that

An Old Hand

Life's not
A puzzle not a game
Eventually you learn
A thing or two
You should have known
When you were 20

    Woman content with nothing

A bad deal

    You'll find the hardest job you ever had
Is coming home

It's tough being enough

Pornography = Exploitation of Men

Homework for husbands
Who remain somehow devoted
To the proposition
It is possible to satisfy 40ish women
In a childish culture
Perhaps well-chosen small appliances
Can do what major purchases
                       have ceased to do

These men spend avid hours
Friday nights
Behind dim Main St. doors
With loosened neckties
                 taking careful breaths
Cruising the aisles
Of video arcades
Blindingly lit hoards
Of modern marvels of communication
Where no one speaks
               more than half a dozen words
Amid shelves stacked
            with produce
From sex factories
          of Florida and California
Small cities in between
Send forth the works
Of amateurish Adams homely Eves
Do-it-yourself de Sades

Efforts that prove
                anything in life
With enough effort
                can be made boring

Jussive or stupefying calisthenics
Offering the emptiest of promises
Invitations to imagine
What has just been actually seen
Is what it is

Not idolatry of flesh
But desperate
Pursuit of possibility denied
By what's already possessed
Is what moves them

Not a prayer
But certainly a wish
So fervent
It jars the deep tectonics of desire
Beyond the boundaries
                of a solitary mind
Beyond the limits
                of this single flesh

A banquet for one withering belief
100 percent American
                and truly human
If anyone has done it
                anything can be done

These men spend money for nothing
Safe sex on the edge
                    of sad discretion

Here are lust's bargains

Movies for men
Who after 20 years
On the same job
Half of their friends laid off
Have modest wants:

Enough to pay the bills
And some left over

A wife who still glows in the dark

Now You Can Worry

Tonight she's wearing her rejection slip
A plotted frumpiness

O you don't know the pain
To look into the midnight eyes
Of that little child
In that picture from El Salvador
That total silence
That premature despair
And feel you can do nothing
Nothing you can do

Tonight she feels so frustrated
She almost cries

I've put up with that woman
For three years
You'd have been proud of me
I didn't turn all black, you know
All red eyeballs, "Now listen Bitch!"
Instead I did it
Like that Larry Davis song
You used to like
"Walk Out Like a Lady"
But I did tell her
Where to put her job

I mean it seems so hopeless
So deeply meant but somehow also false
Crying about retarded whales
Dim-witted dolphins hunting tuna
Who wind up horrifyingly in salads

Sometimes you wonder
Think how the whole world
Is just going to hell
Not just this neighborhood and this house
The *environment*
A world with just
The darkest colors of the rainbow left
As if we try but just can't do enough
God knows, I try.
But anyway, I've decided
To do the little I can do

No sex for you

L'Argent

I know you don't know what
Love is it isn't
Dagwood kisses on the way to work
It's going to work

Love could be but it's not
A 50/50 partnership
Matched sets of polished lies
A usury of affection

I understand that you don't understand
Money don't grow on trees

And if it did,
Those trees would grow
So far away
It would be work to get it

Resistance as Memory

Thinking in Words

Instead of meat
Or any of several barometrically
Possible expressions of fluids
Produced out of flesh, we are drenched
With an intoxicating sympathy
As wonderful as a show business awards banquet

Perhaps in more private
Self-congratulation
We might sit in paneled rooms
And toast ourselves
In Perrier or schnapps

Thinking in strong but well-scrubbed Germanic
Words adopted by romantic conversation
Knowledge of their natural parents lost
To counterfeit a long melodious decay
We might call Art or serious concern

Say, "homeless"

To a young man like me is adventure
Tasty as a bar-b-que sandwich
Melted fat thick on my fingers,
Lips glistening
Pungent aroma curling
Through my whiskers

Thinking up pretty names for the wind
Flirting in the top of oaks across the field
Or swirling in angry like Barbara Stanwyck

Yes—I could call the wind "Barbara"
Or "Miss Stanwyck"
                              No, "Babe"
Now, you can imagine that
Say in urine perception
Bringing us nose up to piss
With the waste of fellow humans?

Wouldn't your lip curl away—
Freedom fighter, weirdo, wino,
Heart-rending refugee or mental case
Only seen clear
When we're properly thinking
In words

So the distinction can be made
Between bar-b-qued felons
And napalmed bystanders
We need to be thinking in words
To tell our hearts and minds
Which way to flutter

As the song says: "No fear, no shame"
As the song says: "Ain't no mountain high enough"
As we scale an Everest of thoughtful
Good intentions, shapely spandex consciences
A myriad glittering categories dancing

Toward a happy day
When nothing liquid or greasy is left
Uncontaminated by our kindness
Once accurately defined
No human
            left untampered with
No slimy duck
            unturned. And laundered.

Like a Tree

—FOR KWAKU PIERCE

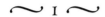 I

The gleaners roll in
With heaped shopping carts

We have constructed ruins
To be reborn out of

Here in our cities, a question
Is there life after birth

∼ II ∼

Cynical innocents
Who think knowledge is dope
Facing the future
With resentful faces
& battery-operated
Primitive art

Throat-slitting music
Martial anthems
For a war on drugs
That scoops up teenage alchemists
Who cook up crack
Who conjure up themselves
Lost

No distant mountainsides, no midnight airdrops
Just sad chumps getting busted on the hottest TV show
Since Allen Funt

~ III ~

There is no vanishing point in our art
Ancestors do not go away

You say they are here
It is not even a question
Of return

Silent and dynamic
A gleaming symmetry of ancestral faces
Smooth African puzzle
That tested
Renaissance mathematics

Ebony or mahogany
Chosen because it is the living color of a man
Matched to the wood carver's own hand

The art is how to
Recognize the spirit
Is the thing you see
These wooden faces looking out
Are not portraits
They are the beings
Who were visiting that tree
When Kwaku found it

Sightseeing in East Texas

These towns are orphans of the Interstate
A slow-motion beauty
Often fires these town squares
With sparks of homely pride
Marvelous stately oaks
Or bright and loved azaleas
Accenting solid buildings
From the 1880s
Which keep, somewhere within,
Bound yellowed scraps
Of what this place has been
That nothing in the Courthouse
Parking slips filled with new cars
Dust-plated pickup trucks
And small-town silences
Even provides a whispered hint
Once happened here

What kind of folks could watch and cherish
Memories of seeing
A man nailed to a tree
Of crimes not hidden in the dark
But planned as carefully with glee
As county fairs or picnics
Hearing wept prayers
And piercing screams turn to mute shock
Brisk bidding sweeps the crowd

For toes and fingers, ears
As flames of hatred
Eddy around numb feet
Then catch a kerosene-soaked cuff
And suddenly,
A human form of flesh and soul
Is drowned in fire?
                    Just us.

Don't think too long
Buckle up your seat belt
And drive on.
We have survived a history that proves
That people, not necessarily humans
Can live without hearts

Psalm

et je suis triste, Seigneur, d'être si triste.
—BLAISE CENDRARS

This morning, cold
Somewhere beyond a single mockingbird
I heard again
A haunting Negro song
Were you there when
They crucified my Lord?

After a decade
Of felons in high places,
Greed unleashed
To herd us into Hell

We're all there now
For lesser crucifixions.

Just another wet East Texas day
Dawn scrubs the sky from darker to light gray

I don't know what to do
I don't know what to do

And all our journalists declare
"The world is mad!"
The same who cried
The end of history in all the streets

The same who yelled "Surf's up!
Democracy is cresting like a tidal wave"
Bringing its flood of common oddities
To all the world
Declare, "The world is mad!"
And have no trouble finding testaments
Rumors, portents and signs
Our people lost in hearts of deserts
Our cities falling from within
Warm valleys white with flames of uprising
Tricksters and traitors
Posing as candidates but well prepared
To fall back on careers
As foul-mouthed comics

We're in the tube, my friends

I don't know what to do
Lord, I don't know what to do

In Kampuchea and South Africa
In middle Europe, Yeats's Ireland, Los Angeles, Somalia
Boys are initiated into death
Before they learn the skill that brought them here

Children completely dipped in numbing pain
Conduct a routine slaughter in the streets
Of innocents and others just like them
Kidnapped into a mindless helical design

I don't know what to do, Lord
I don't know what to do

Here on a slate-gray morning
A cold front comes up from the hill country
Bringing chill rain
Lawmen in 4 x 4s and helicopters
The crack Booze, Butts and Bombs detail
Our square-jawed champions
Until they bite the dust
When suddenly transformed
Soft family men, the best of us
And there's a fund to help
The family

Psychotic prophets
Without the foresight to have booked
A *Passion Play*
End up in re-enactment of the Alamo
A muddy siege
Each dawn both sides count heads and feet
Beneath the thudding racket
Of a sky filled with our journalists
In traffic helicopters

This frenzied passover
Confused with Lent
Catches our breaths like wind
And clouds our faces

If not for a woman's hand,
Peace officers, pacing in high-tech tents
Would send a hundred people to the grave
For bypassed payment of their bullet fees
In carnage more insane than Attica

Thank you for this, O Lord

Thank you O Lord
For the comfort of minute awareness
Our journalists have not forsaken us
Return to tell in microwave Homerics
A vigil that disrupts
The Price Is Right each morning
Just before the Showcase Showdown
But cuts away
Before we miss the end
Who wins the game.

A little charity is what we need
And there's a fund
For pro-life murderers
And funds for milk
Where childhoods blaze and infancies implode
Upon a bed of cinders
Reflected in the dark, round
Always and forever open eyes
Of those made homeless, hopeless
By bombs and guns made in the USA
Properly taxed
Or smuggled by collusion of the law
And slushfund patriots

O Lord, I don't know what to do
I don't like watching what comes into view
I will narrow my eyelids
Till there is nothing in the world but You

WACO, TEXAS, 1993

Back in the Day

When we were boys
We called each other "Man"
With a long *n*
Pronounced as if a promise

We wore felt hats
That took a month to buy
In small installments
Shiny Florsheim or Stacy Adams shoes
Carried our dancing gait
And flashed our challenge

Breathing our aspirations into words
We harmonized our yearnings to the night
And when old folks on porches dared complain
We cussed them out
            under our breaths
And walked away
            and once a block away
Held learned speculations
About the character of their relations
With their mothers

It's true
That every now and then
We killed each other
Borrowed a stranger's car

Burned down a house
But most boys went to jail
For knocking up a girl
He really   truly   deeply   loved
            really   truly   deeply

But was too young
Too stupid, poor, or scared
To marry

Since then I've learned
Some things don't never change:
The breakfast chatter of the newly met
Our disappointment
With the world as given

                    Today,
News and amusements
Filled with automatic fire
Misspelled alarms
Sullen posturings and bellowed anthems
Our scholars say
Young people doubt tomorrow
This afternoon I watched
A group of young men
Or tall boys
Handsome and shining with the strength of futures
Africa's stubborn present
To a declining white man's land
Lamenting
As boys always did and do

Time be moving on
Some things don't never change
And how
          back in the day
Well
          things were somehow better

They laughed and jived
Slapped hands
And called each other "Dog"

Whale Song

You just don't know
How hard it is
To be uncivilized

You think that everyone you eat
Deserves to be eaten

                              Lunch for me
Means someone ain't coming home

So what
If breakfast might have been
The tuna that found a cure for cancer?

Damn sure was tasty!

Songs Without Shadows

It's very good, black brother,
that you sing when you're in doubt
—NICOLAS GUILLÉN

One day
A million years ago
Someone awoke
And found
That sweat and laughter
Had deserted an old friend
The only thing
The desperately still alive
Could do
Was coax the corpse into a fetal Q
And place it in a pit
Hoping to fool some magic
Into thinking their gone friend
Was ready to be born

A lot has happened since
But on this score
There seems to have been no progress
For a million years or more:

We're waiting

One day
Out of a clear blue sky
She says
Our life is at
A crossroads
Our future's
In our hands

Her face was businesslike
But behind her eyes
There was a loaded magazine of tears
She got up and ran to the phone

Collecting estimates for home repairs

One day and one day
After another
Dumb, puzzled rage
I watched my country incinerate my countrymen
In Philadelphia, on a black Mayor's word
City that bears friendship's name
Chorillo shattered
Under pretext of el General's
Illegitimate arrest
Waco, Texas, a few miles from where I live
We watched a televised apocalypse

How can this be? Where will it end?

Stupidity and greed, the right and left hands,
Of a bogus god called Power
Hold us in stern embrace,
Have lashed the world onto a spinning wheel
Of ever more accelerated pain

As if there were surprises
The personality's addiction reappears
Cloud-like simplicity
What can be seen in a face or figure
At the start of all highways
Of songs without shadows,
Of spoken love erasing poetry,
I stand and watch my step

We have mistaken for a possibility our deepest need:
Strength in a woman that is
Soft and warm the natural
Manifold and maybe infinite
Capacity in men for lifelong
And immediate devotion
And have no songs that even whisper
This
Only the din and clatter of a desperate rush
To capture life in the stink of the moment
And hang it in the market-stall for a quick sale

෴

Once I started walking to Saigon
And found a tiny village marketplace
Where an old woman displayed shining things
I left there with a bag of bargains
Viciously bartered candlesticks and platters
Beautifully wrought, melted and hammered
Marvelously shaped from spent shell casings
Made in the USA
That would make lovely presents for my aunts

Each mile I walked, shirt melted to my skin
Was marked by one more treasure left beside the road

I am just a wanderer
I've told you all I know is all I have
To trade or live by
No daily corner calls me at daybreak
But somehow I must live:

I don't know what I will shout in your streets

TENERIFE, ESPAÑA, FEBRERO 1995

The Marks Are Waiting

Our new acuity
Has been misread
As short attention span
But all our aptitude for euphemism
Has been stretched
Like the elastic
In a pair of drawers
Floating around our hips
Uncomfortably
We behold the birth of a new world
Odder than the ones before
In the blue gloom of TV light in Darien
In Pueblo Heights, in College Station
Imagination wilting
Our shopping malls explode with petrojunk
Become necessities
Recycled endlessly
As yellow ribbon

The computers spit out
Inventories of foreshortened amnesia
Long lists of metaphors now obsolete
Willing acceptance of the reprehensible
Lite War
Reports of suffering
Enough to satisfy
But low on passion

You must give up outmoded ideas
New and improved
Marinetti to Super Mario III
Forget
Honor or hygiene
Flushing the planet with
Blood
It's cleaner to think of
Punitive surgery
Competition
Forget it   old hat
Sort of like a lethal Olympics
Strategy   A game of checks
A commerce cruel enough to make E. F. Hutton
Hard sell canard
Shut up but not shut down
Patriotism or the ploy du jour?
The boys in the backroom
Will come up with an ideology
If that still gets it

A 24–7 sideshow
No business but police business
It's never out it's never over
Is what remains, a bit of theater
Going on all the time
A murderous roadshow
With out-of-town tryouts
For smart bombs and stealth politicians
Without a Broadway to go to

If history can still be understood as a record of the deeds of leaders, then the recent history of the United States is the record of bizarre plots and frantic attempts to cover their behinds performed by an amazingly conscienceless batch of born-again hypocrites and felons-in-waiting. Shameless and possibly insane, these men have presided over the decay of both cities and countryside and the demoralization of citizens facing a plummeting standard of living.

If history is properly a narrative of the collective tropism of masses of people, then our recent history is the tale of a populace mesmerized by ever more technically elaborate and intellectually vacuous entertainments designed to distract them from their deepening poverty.

All of the traditional events of the Olympic games are, in fact, martial arts. The rationale of the games, however, is the display of martial prowess in the interest of intertribal nonbelligerence. If these "war games" can, in fact, be construed as simultaneous competition and international cooperation, we have a perfect model for conceptual confusion that can do much more than merely stimulate sales of beer, exercise clothing, and motor vehicles.

For a population addicted to entertainment, demented leaders have invented real war presented as games. The names should be familiar: Grenada, Panama, Kuwait (or Iraq). There are also the minor league games: El Salvador, Nicaragua. Then there's the really funky training camp called Bosnia. Somehow, if you ask folks, you'll find that most people know more details about the 1956 World Series than about any of these campaigns. But each one was presented in the papers and on the radio and TV just like the real thing and—of course—for the unfortunate human beings maimed or killed in those places, it *was* the real thing.

In *Nineteen Eighty-Four*, George Orwell showed how leaders could manipulate populations by preying upon a usefully inarticulate combination of patriotism and self-interest. Ray Bradbury's *Fahrenheit 451* went further in showing the way that scapegoating becomes the instrumentality of such a system. The current permanent crisis provides opportunity for ambitious men to keep busy while thinking they are performing historic deeds; and the public, fitfully distracted by incomprehensible events occurring in never-heard-of places, remains confused. Gore Vidal, educated to find causes for effects, has guessed that the transformation of the United States into a "national security state" in the late 1940s explains the subsequent armed adventures of the past decade, but that means taking these escapades seriously. Actually, the old Roman recipe for ruling is at work: keep the people in line with bread and circuses.

Less bread, more circuses. When there's really nothing worth seeing, the show goes on all night long.

Dirge for Amadou Diallo

It is hard to have your son die
In a distant land

If they said he was a soldier
We would pray
The way we always pray
That his would be the *final* sacrifice
And we would understand

Questions will fill
That churning emptiness
Shaped like a boy
Grown beautifully into a man
There'll be no answers
Still, we'll understand

If he was a true believer
Or a missionary
Apostle or a revolutionary
Ardent altruist or visionary
—in these mean times?
Maybe instead
A hard and nerveless man,
A mercenary
Then we would dread
His noble loss or petty glory
And we would understand

It is hard to have your son die
In a distant land

If accident
Or heart attack
We could blame chance
Or curse our earthbound ignorance
Vow to concoct new mythologies
That wouldn't
Forge us such raw cruelties
Marching our hope
In coffles toward the grave

We'd understand
If someone said he was,
This son, a prodigal:

The kind of man who desperately
Needs the vise of suffering
And hurt and desolation
Some eccentricity to hold him firm
To help him shape his heart
Into an instrument of praise

The kind of man
Who dares to summon whirlwinds
To winnow wisdom from sophistication
O we would wail
And hold our heads
Astonished by the wastefulness of Fate
This repetitious wastefulness of Fate

And understand

But now they tell me
Of a peaceful man
A mother's son, a father's pride
    Seeking to study
In the learned halls
Of a distant, splendid,
Powerful, affluent land
    A young man murdered murdered
And murdered at the hand
Of men sworn to uphold the Law
Not thugs or bandits
    And there's no justice?
There's no recompense?

    O no,
In spite of all our history of terror
In the world
    Uncountable eons of sorrow
Of the world
    O no, O no
We do not understand

    It is hard to have your son die
In a distant land
    And harder still
When we can't understand

An Afternoon with Dr. Blumenbach

. . . yet in the beauty of our Saviour blacknesse is commended,
when it is said, his locks are bushie and black as a Raven.
—SIR THOMAS BROWNE

Light with a veil of dust
Climbs through the window
And pauses to investigate
A shelf of skulls

This new disguise suits me
I think. To probe
To not disturb the Doctor's thoughts
Though I intrude

Methodical and passionless
The Doctor places shot into the scales
Weighing a fragile monument
To breath and sadness

His concentration like a steady flame
Would please Hermes
Bent to a greater task
Than Adam's charge from God
Man to name Man himself
To rank and classify his tribes

The Doctor's sure science
Cannot predict advent of fools

Alfalfa Bill in academic robes
Like Nott and Stoddard

Doctors with heads as empty
As those on his shelf
And hearts as cold as bone

Calling accursed
My own beloved ones
Who dance my tropics
Praising me
Into whose faces
I have signed my name

But in this one I'll invest some time

Of course, my visit cannot take too long
I have more calls to make
A fierce Red poet waits
And then a young American
On Fire Island

I wonder should I beg him to come ride with me
And make a housecall on a troubled century

Crowded with those who cannot even see
The universal skull beneath the skin

Doctor, what must we do
To make them see the light within?

Dangerous Doubts

Dangerous Doubts

The mind invents its own inadequacies
But not the power to erase illusion
That schemes and wholesome dreams
Can become actual despite the truth
That thoughts invest themselves in flesh
And direct motion

That you have 30,000 shots at immortality
But only one you dare not miss at being rich
Or at the least escape the nag of destitution

That maybe exercise shows on TV
Are really harmful
That sound bodies just
Amplify our empty minds

That platitudes contain a grain of wisdom

And fortune's a rush hour train that doesn't wait

To really live means needing other people
That whatever that means love
Could conquer hate

Lustre

What does the warmth
Of your hand mean
That accompanies
The mute slide into sleep
When she feels like a shoemaker's children
All your endearments spent
On lavish wit
Or lyrics mailed away

Trading compliments feels
Like having dinner with strangers
Conversation predicted
The weather, a sadness shared
About the world today
(Art) (land) (livestock) auction prices
The polished surface of civility

Is this warmth ardor or a vital sign?
Bad married love or good
Clairvoyance
Your hand   your heart
The hot comb in the radio
That pulled Glenn Miller's Orchestra
Out of the sky

Cameo in Sudden Light

How possibly could I
Fall in love with you
From looking at the back of your
Head
The care of studious hands
Shadowed curls
One broken sequin
Glittering and hiding
On gray carpeted step
Rustle of an intruding word
In a sea of paper, full of words
Fading and slowly writhing
Like traders of fable
In a haunted green quadrant
Carefully natural and tended
Tourista allure
A 2-foot stack of powdering disasters,
Yellowing pathos, wrinkled household
Hints
Frayed recipes and task force reports
Of one dowdy crisis after another
Discovered the deed
Costing into the thousands
As the shy light of a lost sequin
Blurts into fuchsia anxiety
No, I don't want you to see me

We are stealing avalanches of light

These several things
Seeking glimmers of focus
Each in our part of the room
Hiding and shining
Kuji Kiri the Ninja technique
Of performing hypnotic hand movements
Sha   the 5th center of power
Opening the Eight Psychic Channels
Begins at the base of the balls
Flows to the solar plexus
Tu Mo the base of the spine
Jen Mo at home in your brain
The body is one ocean
After another, secret and blue
Holding treasures when you have mastered
This motion

Much is promised
Power
Is useful only when
She hides her face
Within the shadow of a jeweled hand
When she beckons
A mystic light in Bermudian waters
A potted tree that forces you
To cross gleaming lobbies
To prove that the blossoms are silk
And abject poverty and ingenuity

And love of beauty
Will steer our troubled course
As long as there are sad-faced maidens
Bending and shaping flowers in Taiwan
We are bright and alive in our security
Gasping as if rocketing upward
Out of travel brochure blue
Is not of the much that is promised

Amusing wall shadows are included
Attract popular and becoming friends!
High side those who once snubbed you!
Strange and colorful phonecalls
Will come to you from unpronounceable places!
But power is one thing you won't get

How could I
Possibly
Go on this way
Without you
At least sending some
Some discreetly placed
Signal
Seal it
With the voice of a seashell
The whorl of a conch
Or gleam of ancilla
Salvager,
For God's sake
Turn around

Country Song

Don't know a thing
Except what I know:
I like great big legs
& where they go

I love the colors in the Arkansas sky
When the sun goes down
And I'm as lonely as an empty chair
When you're not around

Multicultural

Watch who ends up in contestant's row
I like it when the colored people win
It always was all women years ago
Once in a while maybe a young Marine
LCpl in dress uniform
Every other word he said was "sir"
Probably a newlywed on top of that
You know he's going to win a car
Or bedroom suit
Not that the game is fixed but to be fair
I'm sure someone at CBS
Made lots of money figuring this out
Before I did
The way they've got it now
All kinds of people get to come on down
OK by me. But yet and still
I like it when the colored people win

Low Rider

Kind of guy
                         who wants 3 kids
Loves being "Popi!"
May be a reluctant groom
     like most sane men

An ideal husband
                              if she understands
His wildness and dictatorship
And all his pride
          except her & the kids

Is dancing in that loud garage
& all those intense hours
Making his lime-green Malibu
Trace perfectly the daft *dressage*
Of a distracted Colonel's
Most haughty palomino

For more
                    How to Keep Peace in Your Home
See our
            next installment

An Even-Tempered Girl Holds Her Breath

He looked for mischief
But he only found
Tantrums so slight
They wouldn't register
On any instrument
Less finely gauged
Than she in time
Tuned him to be

Um hmm

She holds her breath
A beat

If he forget me, I could disappear
Like this

Silently fading and slowly
Like an ancient VistaVision movie
Shown very late at night
So ineptly lensed
The only evidence of lovers seen
One nose and one nose
On each edge of the TV screen
As they are heard
Talking, dramatically pledging

Or better yet, *he* could

mmmm Huhnh!

She Lived to Be 100

—ORIKI FOR WILLIAM A. THOMAS,
HIS GOODNESS AND STRENGTH

The first person I ever knew
who died
The last I can recall
to exit dreaming
The whole house knew
something was wrong
That morning
Broad daylight stood
in every window
Boldly shining
And he was still
in bed in his pajamas

A Kind of Accounting

Habana and the pretty ocean
Then Miami
Each stop a little less Spanish
And then LaGuardia

My Uncle Robert large and handsome
As the sun itself   on the tarmac
Resplendent in a pinstripe suit
And camel benny
Shrugged on his shoulders Russian Jewish style
Huge enough to fling   bold toreador
Around my dad's whole little family

Expansive gesture

But he wouldn't lend his brother money
And ridiculed his job
When he finally found one

He said "I didn't get what I got
Through bad investments"
Then made a half a dozen
Right away   as years went by

But every New Year's Eve
Always at Robert's lavish Harlem party
Warmed

Full of greens black-eyed peas VO and Redd Foxx records
The brothers compared notes
Laughing & fully armed with wary candor
Watching each other prosper in New York

Cute Girl with a Toy Monkey

Looks like the girl I loved
When I was young
Whose name   whose name
    is on the tip of my tongue
But it doesn't matter

She was the generic one
The one that was perfect
For me

Does she look like an angel?
No. She looks like a girl

Rapt in calm concentration
Peacefully. Transported on thought

I can't imagine her being loud
Well, except under certain circumstances

Her sparkling eye light
And pursed lips
She's either very happy with herself
Or nuts

So beautiful!

I change for the F train at Roosevelt
And watch her
        gliding away
But at 71st and Continental
Here she is again!
        boarding my train

The girl that is perfect for me
That I never got

When I looked for Beatrice
I found you

When I looked for Eurydice
I found you

When I wasn't looking for anybody at all
I found you

That's what, Fate?

Flash Point

This useless clairvoyance
Is embarrassing
What good is it to know
The motives behind manners

And worse, the so what stares
Of those upon whom you manage
To inflict this wisdom

There is more space
Awaiting exploration
More clouds of gas
That need their picture took

God Sends Love Disguised as Ordinary People

We never quite could tell
    strength from stupidity
Pride in perseverance
The point where stubbornness
Purchased a harvest of futility

If the body has forgotten how to sleep
    what chance has thought
To teach it subtleties
Like tenderness or faith

All that could matter
    is the reciprocating warmth
Of flesh—wordless and beyond translation
    to idea or category
Nothing numerical and yet
Not boundless, either
Nothing so grand or abstract

In other words,
    we were not brutes for lack of feeling
Nor sorrowful in spiteful isolation
Not lonely yet
But damaged by avoiding touch
Being only smart enough to trust
That there's some
    gifted outcast family

Somewhere a troop of *djalis*
That still performs the music that we need
To reconnect our feet to dirt
To fling our arms like windmills
Spinning in dusted twilight

The point being not that you beat
    yourself up appreciating
What so and so has done for you
But that you finally remember
You've been her gypsy, too

Magnetic Charms

I'm saying
        I have outgrown promises
Not you

Call it
Reality   because there is
  no better word

To call our secrets
Falsity   that haunts us
With the fear
That what we know and hide
Is all we are

But if false actions
       haunt us
What faith
    Old women in small villages
    in backward lands
Could possibly find resonance
In words?

When I touch you
That zone of heat
Beneath my hand—
Trust that

  What do you call
     a trouble shared
  Check "strength" or "weakness"

The cancer patients
        smoking on the patio, for instance

Incorrigibles
Roaring, indignant, daring the world's end
With love of laughter
As if to say
"We lived and live our lives
                this way
And won't regret it
            even when we change"

I do not think that I can
Guarantee the truth
By plan or force of will

And fear that disappointing you
        will undo me
Not you

What I have given in majestic arrogance or quiet need
Does it glow in you?

Does it calm or warm
Or furnish afternoons with peaceful hours?

I am the one I do not wish
        to leave bereft
Not you

I'm saying

The last time I walked on Lake Conroe
It kind of gave way

Equinox

It was an act of stealth / And troubled pleasure
—WORDSWORTH, *THE PRELUDE* (1850)

~ I ~

There may be other roles you recognize
      Sailors at nightwatch
Soldiers on picket

But we are shepherds now
And it is Spring!

    And we are talking . . .

OK, so we're not shepherds
But this is useful play

Like shepherds on a dark hillside
Drawing lines between the stars,
   We reach beyond ourselves
To meet ourselves

Or are we talking
Just to fill the space between us
   To get over
A century that ends
   in fireworks
And worldwide efforts
To undo the future?

Then we were dancing . . .

This is my real life.
The day is still wet
    from morning's rain
Pavements begin to steam

Killer 1970s guitars
    rattling the dash
Driving west into a majolica landscape
the city in the rearview
    clasped by night
Abandoned by the sun

At best, a graveyard chance
    "Time to get your grip
& move on . . ."

¡O preach us some pleasant nonsense,
    Por favor!

Amuse us, O Lord!
    We are the audience
For your sneak preview
    of Heaven!

Thrust into this florid maze,
Trust curiosity
To find its way
To cleverness

A long-waited legion of idolators
Arriving after giddy pilgrimage

Then came the prismed vision
As we saw the world through tears

 II

No, it is Spring!

Three days of rain,
    not Biblical
But more than this ground
Could take

Standing water everywhere

After 3 days of rain
They look like lakes
These fields near Hockley
    fields waiting for cotton
Corn or soy
Tract homes or condominiums
    Or little malls
Glimmering like fish-scales in the sun
As a sheet of egrets settles in
    beside the lakes
That will not be here
    in three days
In fields that will not be here
    in three years

But we were talking . . .

Shepherds,
Or boys at useful play

You find the married men at 4 o'clock
Leaning against their trucks
    beside the road
Sharing half-pints or 6-packs
Or, in the city, at a cocktail lounge
Trying to prolong the day's escape

But there are others
    who are not here
Men
Who have years to speak of
Farmers, retired mechanics

Old men gather at breakfast
To direct the day into its starting gate
Booting the sun along a slotted course
Above the never-ending shadow puppet dance of power
The energetic pettiness of mundane business

These high priests of expected disappointments
Raise their polyphonic song:
Life is unpleasant   but predictable

If this is solace,
These men standing
    up against the wall

These are the guardians
Of future pathways—

But it is Spring!

~ III ~

You feel like skipping
But the costume
Wants a more processional step

Will there be ruins where we walk?
Will our footfalls echo purposes?

Count this, if not as blessing
Then as a good thing:

Talking together as gray-haired men
      with the guy
You looked up at the stars with
When you were boys

And wondering if there's a God
      a girl, a goal
A meaning to the universe
& knowing now
      you really do not know much more
Than you did back then,

These conversations
Like a diamond's facets

Like sunlight on fields suddenly made lakes
The subject always the same
Yet seems transparently
Deflecting something deeper
More personal—demanding
More attention
When you think it over
As you will, inventing
What you should have said
Too late for that now
And next time will be deceiving

A boy's job
To listen to the old men's lies
And learn the music . . .

> *A boy's job is*
> *To listen to the old men lie*
> *& learn the music . . .*

I never been nowhere
Where the old Blues singers been

But I swear to my soul
I don't want to go there again

Back-Ordered Tears

It was when neon was no longer available
That they went mad.
There was nothing to cut the Formica.
Offbeat shouting dirty words
Dropping glitter on backward lands
Nothing seemed to help.

It was quarter to 2 in a small, dull town
Jukebox exhausted, coffee burned stale
A go-go girl sluffs on her bedroom slippers
Punches some feeling back into her thighs.

It was in those days musicians started dancing
Didn't have to touch their instruments.
In fact, they couldn't even stop the music playing
It was so much sadness in the world.

Other titles of interest from Coffee House Press

That Kind of Sleep by Susan Atefat Peckham

it was today by Andrei Codrescu

A Handmade Museum by Brenda Coultas

Maraca: New and Selected Poems 1965–2000 by Victor Hernández Cruz

The Cloud of Knowable Things by Elaine Equi

*Notes on the Possibilities and Attractions of Existence:
Selected Poems 1965–2000* by Anselm Hollo

Legends from Camp by Lawson Fusao Inada

Teducation by Ted Joans

Cranial Guitar by Bob Kaufman

You Never Know by Ron Padgett

The Magic Whip by Wang Ping

Earliest Worlds by Eleni Sikelianos

Foreign Wife Elegy by Yuko Taniguchi

Transcircularities: New and Selected Poems by Quincy Troupe

In the Room of Never Grieve: New and Selected Poems 1985–2003 by Anne Waldman

Word Group by Marjorie Welish

Available at fine bookstores everywhere.

Good books are brewing at coffeehousepress.org.

Coffee House Press is a nonprofit literary publisher
supported in part by the generosity of readers like you.
We hope the spirit of our books makes you seek out
and enjoy additional titles on our list.
For information on how you can help bring great literature
onto the page, visit coffeehousepress.org.

Funder Acknowledgments

Coffee House Press is an independent nonprofit literary publisher. Our books are made possible through the generous support of grants and gifts from many foundations, corporate giving programs, individuals, and through state and federal support. This project received major funding from the National Endowment for the Arts, a federal agency. Coffee House Press has also received support from the Minnesota State Arts Board, through appropriations by the Minnesota State Legislature and by the National Endowment for the Arts; and from the Elmer and Eleanor Andersen Foundation; the Buuck Family Foundation; the Bush Foundation; the Grotto Foundation; the Lerner Family Foundation; the McKnight Foundation; the Outagamie Foundation; the John and Beverly Rollwagen Foundation; the law firm of Schwegman, Lundberg, Woessner & Kluth, P.A.; Target, Marshall Field's, and Mervyn's with support from the Target Foundation; James R. Thorpe Foundation; West Group; the Woessner Freeman Foundation; and many individual donors.

This activity is made possible in part by a grant from the Minnesota State Arts Board, through an appropriation by the Minnesota State Legislature and a grant from the National Endowment for the Arts.

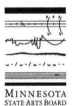

MINNESOTA
STATE ARTS BOARD

NATIONAL
ENDOWMENT
FOR THE ARTS

To you and our many readers across the country, we send our thanks for your continuing support.

Good books are brewing at coffeehousepress.org